T0088444

BOB CHILCOTT

SUN DANCE

from *Organ Dances*

MUSIC DEPARTMENT

OXFORD
UNIVERSITY PRESS

Sun Dance

(from *Organ Dances*, for organ and orchestra)

BOB CHILCOTT
(b. 1955)

I Chorus coupled to Ped.
II Chorus coupled to I
III Solo reed

Rhythmic and spiky (♩ = *c.*144)

This piece is a slightly modified version of the fifth movement from *Organ Dances*, for organ solo, strings and percussion.

© Oxford University Press 1997

Printed in Great Britain

OXFORD UNIVERSITY PRESS, MUSIC DEPARTMENT, GREAT CLARENDON STREET, OXFORD OX2 6DP

The Moral Rights of the Composer have been asserted. Photocopying this copyright material is ILLEGAL.

marcato
Solo (III)
f

sub. p
cresc. poco a poco
cresc.
cresc.
cresc.

ff
add

add

Un poco meno mosso
I
mp più legato e espressivo
mf legato
II
II to Ped.

I
I to Ped.
II
dim.
– I to Ped.

dim.
Tempo primo
dim.
I to Ped.
f
I
f

marcato
Solo (III)
f

I
sub. p

cresc. poco a poco

cresc.
cresc.
cresc.
Full ff
+III
+III
ff